BARKING
in the
WIND

BARKING
in the
WIND

Conflict With Human Apathy

V. Mezzatesta

iUniverse, Inc.
Bloomington

BARKING IN THE WIND

iUniverse books may be ordered through booksellers or by contacting:

iUniverse
1663 Liberty Drive
Bloomington, IN 47403
www.iuniverse.com
1-800-Authors (1-800-288-4677)

ISBN: 978-1-4620-3923-4 (sc)
ISBN: 978-1-4620-3958-6 (ebk)

Printed in the United States of America

iUniverse rev. date: 07/25/2011

CONTENTS

[We must find a positive, balanced solution that will mutually benefit human and non-human welfare equally while preserving both parties integrity . . .]

Dedicated to all my four-legged champions and all those liberators who struggle with both success and despair in their loyal and selfless service for the defense of the voiceless . . . for they equally exude loyalty and love in their hearts . . .

ABOUT THE BOOK

Few people understand the difficulties animal rights activists undergo. Some regard them as extremists or eccentric; rebels or ridiculous. Either way, the activists battle through all the human apathy and ignorance to reveal their good intentions; to be a voice to the voiceless and protect the defenseless. This book gives the public a true rendition of how some of us endure many obstacles while attempting to change the public outlook on animal and human coexistence. Until the human populous stops referring to animals as "property", very little will be accomplished in the fight to preserve animal dignity, welfare and protection. Yet the battle will never cease until mankind realizes the threat on overall humanity, should we give up on our animal friends; domestic, farm and wild. There are both positives and negatives within the various animal rights groups while each can reveal to us effective and unique end results toward the goal of animal liberation. Great strides will be made yet at a cost that many activists will inevitably bear . . . all in the name of liberation . . .

INTRODUCTION

How did barking about injustices within the animal kingdom become too loud and incoherent that folks can't even heed what is being vocalized? Has all of our aggressive internal battles and "bull-biting" at one another clouded the real objectives here? Our goals are to eradicate animal cruelty and get public support, not to destroy the few progresses we've already achieved. My dogs can bark, wag their tails happily at the neighbors, dig up the yard, never travel a straight line, and manage to effectively chase out vermin, and still find they are welcomed with loving and open hearts. Tolerance is an attribute that unfortunately is not found in many people. Tolerance of an idea or way of life suggests that there is a decision to take an action: to accept or to not, to explore the option or to dismiss it. Somewhere along the line tolerance became a suggestion that has been associated with animal rights-it is not a suggestion, it is an essential. Fundamentally we have to take action against these negative ideologies and take a few notes from the animals. We could learn a lot from a dog when engaging the public in regards to animal welfare. Are we projecting ourselves in a positive light? Are we sounding off with the right message? Are we targeting the right viewers with the right tools? Or, are we taking a straight line path to nowhere? Injustices will not be tolerated. My personal challenges will give others a "reality check" at some of the successes and pitfalls that come with animal lovers' targeting community indifferences. I take the "muzzle" off and give not only an indifferent society an "up close and personal" look into my world but the many "bunny huggers" (a term that outside community uses to describe animal rights activists such as "tree huggers" for environmentalists) out there an accurate account as well. A commonality many activists share is that as long as there are inhumanities and indifferences toward our animal friends, our war in their defense will never cease . . . no matter the consequences. Those words are paraphrases from the champions that truly put non-human animals' welfare before themselves. In reality, many aggressive acts such as plotting midnight rescues from a research facility or setting fire to a fur farm result in those heroes that no longer walk this planet a free individual. He or she, no longer has the tools to continue the cause. In the waging war against the senseless too little effort is being exerted. It is like fighting a war with a slingshot instead of bazooka in your enormous war with little change resulting in counter-effectiveness; the voiceless suffers equally. We must find a positive, balanced solution that will mutually benefit human and non-human welfare equally while preserving both parties integrity. I present my own experiences and infuse it with a satirical style all my own to give you as unbiased a picture as possible in my efforts to save our animals; domestic, farm and wild alike. After an accurate picture has been painted of the battleground we are all in, I will give you some resources of ammunition to join us in this epic fight-then perhaps we can finally do more than just bark in the wind . . .

CHAPTER 1

Failures leave a nasty scar behind

Our societies actions, failures and shortcomings need to be examined before any solutions can be discussed. To effectively offer solutions to a problem you  must effectively identify the problem. Then, we can move to the positives and discuss strategies to win them over. Every strong activist can tell you that the physical and emotion scars they have acquired were interregnal in making them the activists they are today. Society is being bombarded with so much negative publicity in regards to the activists that something must be changed so we all "play nice in the sandbox" together, so to speak. In fact, I assure you they will "pick up their toys" and run home! Too often, we only see them (the activists) portrayed as common terrorists with baseless agendas such as burning down some long standing research group thought to be looking for a human cure. We are blinded to the entire story because narrow focused media fail to reveal all the facts; thus intentionally taking the attention away to the defenseless animals being mutilated and disfigured in the process. We have to stop telling half of the story and give the activists a chance to tell the truth . . . the whole story! Both sides need to be told equally for the public to gain a better understanding and give way to tolerance. As humanitarian activists, we cannot continue to employ the brute force tactic we have been employing. If you do the same thing you have always done, you will continue to get the same result. Speaking thunderous to a person who doesn't understand the language you are speaking does nothing for effective communication. This is the same concept that can be applied to those in our society who may have sensitive ears when approaching the subject of animal rights. There are major differences of opinions in what cruelty is and what is not. Discipline comes in all forms but should be tempered with good judgment and positive reinforcement. I know, I know . . . you may say the positive approaches are rarely used with the animals when something goes wrong. Where did the positives kick in when little Oscar pees on the new carpet and the owner shoves his nose in it and leaves him permanently outside, never to mingle with the family again? When do folks consider Oscar in any decision making processes in a typical household setting where he apparently was to "coincide" with the human family he was adopted into for the rest of his life? Did we forget the positive approaches here and is this the positive or negative. I will side with the latter. Some tactics work and some don't; all dependent of the situation handed to you.

Ok then, so what makes you think we (Oscar and all his other little friends) are invincible? Don't you know that if someone cuts your face, you will bleed too and . . . badly? I suppose you think that it doesn't hurt when "Joe Citizen" slices and serves me up as salami! And yet we (along with the defenseless animal) still find the way to survive and try to adapt, continue on, battle scars and all. Before we activists teach others though, we must learn from our own tragedies and mistakes and try not to dig ourselves in a hole we can't get out of. I am certain if both activists and the rest of the society understood some of my hardships, as an activist and as "Josephine Citizen", the realization that being that one "voice and protector" of our animal friends is quite an arduous undertaking and a demanding mission. After examining what both roles entail, perhaps then a point of view can be seen that allows society to empathize with the everyday bias an activist is faced with and with these injustices leave scars proving no one is immune to pain. Moreover, a true to the core activist will testify to the sentiment that roadblocks are inevitable, The way around the road block and the possibility that lies ahead is the driving force behind any action. The voice for the voiceless is the ultimate mission and whatever or whoever lies in the path of the righteous will witness the determination that true to the core activists harbor. Not only will you find that you must lean on your fellow man for a source of strength to continue the battle; those animals out there have no one else to speak out for them if you do end your campaign because of a little "bump in the road!"

They said "Walk the Human"...
Never said anything about bringing them back!

Ok, how does my world look outside looking in? Do my views and past experiences mold my present perceptions of

4

those around me? Of course they do! Walls of negative experience seem to have been built; cemented by dismissing attitudes around me. Yet in still I continue to imagine that one day society will cease referring to animals as mere "property" as an attainable goal. Awe, I live in a fantasy world . . . wishing for world peace and all! Why do activists and animal lovers like myself, continue to step in it with bare feet? How can my enormous efforts in saving humanity end up chopping me down to size? They "say" they care, but every step I take in aggression; two steps are pounded out of me to turning us into the hypocritical powers that we have been waging this war against. To defend the abused and neglected and to be the "voice of the voiceless", our barking simply cannot fall on deaf ears. If it does, all we have accomplished in repairing these antiquated, societal ignorance's will be in vain thus we ourselves promote indifference and fear. Taking the risks to help ensure that the animals do have a voice and breaking from the norms, we are belittled and reduced to worms . . . slithering into a hole in attempts to maintain our own preservation. If we are not careful though, the process of changing opinions and cruel habits many times lead to disappointments because of slow or ineffective courses of actions thus eventual destruction of the very laws of humanity we originally intended to change.

Sure, I go into a defensive posture when those figurative knives get thrown at me by the very humans that I seek answers. I want to instinctively resort to the "for every action there is an equal and opposite reaction" when I hear of an injustice and my retaliatory measures fail. Rhetoric is all I hear; thoughtless public interests so called selfish agendas calling to half-assed attention to their human egos and the need to overpower the defenseless. I live each day on this earth to make known how this so called "educated society" is destroying the livelihood of the animals they proclaim to protect.

Without conscience, we are standing idly by as the public inhumanely herd, extinguish and exploit those (animals) who wish nothing but to coexist peacefully with their human counterparts. Today's humans test, breed, entrap, and manipulate a so-called, "beautiful and magnificent" creature and in the same breath, slaughter him/her and their young inhumanely for vanity, profit or science.

"Animals' worse threats are predators not of the
animal kind but of the human . . ."

I watch countless authority who contradict their own literary writings and religious beliefs as they inhumanly abuse and demean the very creatures they profess to protect. The abusers who were never held accountable for their atrocities are causing the liberators to take matters in their own hands all across the globe. They opt to demolishing man-made structures that entrap animals indefinitely, release the wild back to countryside, and even free a defenseless beast from heavy chains that choke the very life and livelihood out of them. We interpret acts of these " . . . save the day!" liberation movements as unjust and terroristic? We are mislead to believe current policies in place are "protective" measures though countless researchers find the majority of "our" acts are in fact, increasing violence and negative behaviors amongst our animal communities. We place laws for example to chain and cage animals we feel dangerous to the public when in fact measures of this kind only create more unpredictable and dangerous behaviors.

Chaining domestic dogs account for more vicious attacks on residents within our society today than those unchained and in proper fenced in enclosures proven countless times by dozens of reputable organizations. Though this one example has been time and time proven, we allow our officials to use these laws to avoid the very problem they were attempting to reduce; vicious dog attacks in the communities.

Additionally, we find our fathers before us designed and genetically "engineered" (still practiced) the domesticated creature to ultimately fail without our human involvement; if left as nature intended (as wildlife), they would have had better survival skills. One of the most common examples is the domestic canine. If left alone hundreds of years ago, he (the domesticated dog) would not have all the physical and mental issues facing them today. Mankind markets/engineers creatures that were once a thriving independent animal being to an over-bred, inbred and overpopulated withering species of unstable weaklings; mere scavengers pleading for human companionship. Another example of failing policies related to our domesticated animals are "Breed Specific Legislation" or BSL being put into place in the name of citizen protection from vicious attacks. Society designs breeds to fail but don't realize breeds such as pit bulls are designed by humans; trained, over-bred and inbred to foster vicious and uncontrollable behavior. Additionally, humans have subjected the pit bull to numerous acts of cruelty and abuse from owners to include long term tethering, fighting them in rings and countless forms of abuse causing these breeds to become a harm humans. We (humans) are directly responsible for the dangers yet turn around and blame the animal by exterminating the lot. I don't have one perfect answer to solve every problem affecting animal welfare. On that same line, I can't wave my "super-activist "cape around and somehow make the pains go away. I do know, however, it's a combination of many actions by more than just one human being. I have lived through the challenges in the pursuit of selfless service in defense of our animal friends.

> *"If you think you have 1st Amendment Rights, you are sadly misled . . .*
>
> *You have rights only when it suits "human" causes, not animals!"*

Only those activists that have been through defeat would understand my occasional pains defending my beloved animal friends. When I (an average animal lover and activist) tell folks that a simple act of chaining a dog for indefinite periods as an act of terrorism and we must retaliate, I am looked upon as unstable and perhaps some homegrown terrorist myself. It's horrendous to witness countless acts of malice and not be able to openly project your feelings or act against them leading us to understand . . . This is not a nation of so called "freedom of speech." I have been persecuted both by threats and even disassociation by my own peers for thoughts. When I hear of some heroic liberators destroy some lab that used animals as test subjects, I actually feel joy knowing one less facility out there is in business to torture my animal friends. Yet saying that out loud has got coworkers and superiors monitoring my every move and no doubt on some terrorist watch list. I've done the familiar acts of petitioning, pushed for tougher laws, engaged in verbal threats, and reporting illegal and inhumane actions to authorities responsible for handling such matters but nothing seems to be "enough" in my eyes. I've exposed the wrongs-doings by my own neighbors through video segments and subsequently faced threats of termination by my superiors. "Hey, I only reported the fact, that's all!" I wish I was one of the soldiers who liberate animals that plot some rescue operation in the middle of the night and freed hundreds of rabbits, or rats, or even monkeys from inevitable torture and death. I have to remind myself every day, not everyone can be "Invincible" and be some super-anarchist. I promise you one thing . . . I'm applauding their actions. I know everyone can't be that one heroic martyr and sacrifice everything . . . I advocate the "walk-the-walk" and somehow find myself feeling inadequate. I feel anxieties that almost interfere with my productivity both on and off work. I've become so paranoid and insecure in so many facets. Every day I fear even driving to work for I might run into a stray or see a chained dog inside a neighbor's fenced in yard. Even an unfortunate squirrel that's found his untimely death by a nameless driver would terrorize me inside. I've become an emotional wreck. I cry uncontrollably if I see Sarah McLaughlin on the commercials for ASPCA ®; her songs throw me into a secret depression. Oh, don't pretend it doesn't stab you right in the heart too now! I stood in utter disbelief when I saw the little fish in a major department store in pint-sized bags, alone, motionless and looking pitiful and hungry . . . waiting to be sold or placed in some fish tank to be stared at by some thrill seeking passerby.

I wonder how many of my fellow activists can say they face major flack from their workplace; thus constantly subjected to cruel animal related jokes and hunting stories? I endure folks at work laudably discussing some unconscionable act against a dog or cat like it was just "another piece of news." I hear a colleague speak smugly taking their "rescued" puppy to the vet because the little fellah was having trouble breathing . . . only to discover the blame lay on their shoulder because the pup's collar was too tight. Yeah, that doesn't suppose to get any rise out of me, of course not! Somehow they couldn't realize a puppy grows therefore needs to be checked daily? How many (including me) are right now thinking that there should be an I.Q. test given to folks to procreate (children) or adopt a companion animal . . . hmmm? Though I internalize my disdain, I outwardly continue to promote positive ways to help them with their personal animal issues. I'm ironically known as some sort of "dog lady" to come to for advice and referrals to my department. I regularly submit safety and animal welfare tips throughout our local and work community. I've even reached to the public through personal websites and public speaking engagements. Not a few weeks after the choking puppy incident, that same individual takes

12

the very same rescued puppy and drops him off to the pound; obviously too much responsibility, seeing how the puppy was for a self-serving vanity/fulfillment in the first place. Oh well, another little guy on their way to euthanasia. No big deal to them. After all, it's just an animal not worthy of human kindness . . . It's "property". Try interacting with monsters every day at work and hold your tongue. And the average uneducated citizen sees me the enemy? I could argue, they (these heartless individuals) mean little to me anyway if this is their mindset. However, it certainly does nothing to improve the environment. How do we as activist attempt to lighten our disdain and cynicism towards the indifferent society? And we have the public thinking *we* are the "bad guys" . . . perhaps an error? Amazing enough perceptions are clouded and we have to work around that and find a tactical way to recover each day; in the interest of those who have no voice in the matter.

CHAPTER 2

Methodology, at best, situational!

To effectively succeed in mending societal hypocrisies and indifferences, we must engage in more systematical and tactical processes (discussed in later chapter). Before we take on such a heavy task, people out there must understand the methodology behind animal endangerment and how it may or may not contribute to the overall effectiveness in combating all aspects of animal endangerment, not just one single area. With this said, each situation will reveal concepts that may help you to understand activists approaches working in these tremendous conditions. Then, move forward while airing on the side of caution when facing personal challenges. Let's shed some light on some "methods of attack" and the advantages and disadvantage of each . . .

The "Freedom Fighter" Wolf

The "freedom fighter" has always been an effective way to cause "shock and awe"; if this is the "intended" outcome. Yet the freedom fighters have both their positives and negatives and are effective in certain situations perhaps. It seems to have its place when all other means fail. It's kind of like using the "whatever means necessary" when all other actions didn't free the poor "lab monkey" from imminent destruction. However, it has its drawbacks and limitations attached in the scope of fighting for animal liberation. Never would I personally discriminate or deter people from these acts of aggression, however, it takes a certain personality to act in this revolution; to fight the "establishment." Aside from being very dangerous to both you and the animals, typically, these are the individuals that are unafraid of losing everything in their own selfless service to human/non-human rights. It is usually those young, single, lone wolves who have very little material possessions or wealth. Or, many tend be small "packs" of perhaps 3 to 10 exuberant individuals that don't seem to conform to societal norms very well and have nothing to lose. No matter the cost, they are willing to be incarcerated for their acts of humanitarianism. They fight with unyielding zeal. It is the ones we "passive aggressive" activists revere. Non-believers to the cause deem their measures as acts of terrorism. Though their (freedom fighters) intent is to save animals in eminent danger may be an immediate success, freedom fighters risk losing their battle facing potential elimination and future consequences. A decrease soldiers' in numbers negates the totality of threat to society. We stand to lose another dynamic warrior in our cause; never again to be utilized in future rescues. "Major players" ultimately end up being "locked up." Operations could be foiled by informants, saboteurs or even by simple lack of organization. Missions are spontaneous at best and directed to a single humanitarian cause . . . worst case scenario . . . as stated earlier, a dead hero to read about in future manifestos. Whether it is a dairy farm abusing cows or the guy across the street leaving their puppy out in the cold, all the warrior for animal rights are concerned with is that no one is out there saving them and they alone are their only hope for survival. Waiting on the "red tape", which often times slows the legal process, is not going to solve the immediate threat to that particular herd or the one animal out there soon to starve and/or freeze to death. The Freedom Fighters now become a short-term fix for a long-term problem.

There are those who argue saving one little guy (dog, cat, hamster, etc.) is not worth the efforts that so many animal lovers are willing to take risk to save. They (the individual fighting for animal rights) watch sometimes helpless and stare across the fence at the neighbor who has a scrawny chained up Labrador barely fed and ignored by the very folks that adopted the dog in the first place from the local shelter. Since this particular dog is being fed and has some meager doghouse that fall within "code" with bowls of days-old and almost stagnant water, the local Animal Control doesn't make any arrests due to owners following the bare minimums of the law. So, this is ok to let the dog remain lonely and chained, with no one to play ball with or come in from the shivering temperatures. Since laws concerning animal welfare are many times insufficient, vague and regard animals as mere property, very few changes have been made in decades and unfortunately we find a large population of humans see no problems within this arena. That one neighbor that screams and pitches massive campaigns to save these poor little ones are looked at as overzealous and radical. These super-humans trying to save them typically argue their position through a famous quote . . .

"The humanity you show for a dog may not save the world . . .but it means the world to that ONE dog"
—author unknown

One rabbit, two rabbits or a hundred, no matter the number, each one is significant to them (as I tend to agree), yet some instances result in a whole bunch of beloved critters in almost the same situation . . . in homeless, crowded shelters, or placed with individuals that have little or no means or common sense to properly care and sustain them. What exactly do you now do with a hundred rabbits you freed from a lab while executing these mission unseen by the law? Do all of the furry critters reach "never never land?" Or, do some get "rounded up" by some local overcrowded organizations that already take on too much both physically and financially? Where do they go? Communities barely are equipped for what they rescue from day to day. Are we dismissing their heroic efforts, no? We just have to be able to have long-range strategies to counteract the foreseeable problems these acts may cause. So, the freedom fighters are limited in scope, character and longevity. Freedom fighters can only be "actively" engaged within limits and with unconstrained resources and power to support such huge and risky feats of heroism. I know one thing . . . that one "lab rat" is forever gracious!

The Passive-Aggressor" Sheepdog

I can readily say that many activists, no matter the platform, fall into this category. In fact, the strength in numbers within this primary category tends to do quite well. Though this is one of the most "widespread" courses of action, the aggressors mistakenly tend to consider these folks in a very negative tenor until some thought given to the subject. Freedom fighters initially view these guys as the ones sitting in "the bleachers" and not having the intestinal fortitude to go the distance. When in actuality, the non-aggressors and passive aggressors frequently stand very close to the scenes funding and/or facilitating the freedom fighting "grandstanders" in their "night ops". Oh wait though, the average citizen likes these mild mannered "advocates." They can feel gratification knowing we are fighting for animal rights using more conservative measures. However, It is naïve to seriously believe, that those small, tactical, groups of freedom fighters were capable of funding this massive rescue operation with "no change in their wallet" and with absolutely no involvement from the "sheepdogs!" True, some of the radical groups came from some wealthy background, but in reality, many are funded behind the scenes by, of course folks . . . the passive aggressive "sheepdogs". Money drives the train in almost every situation known to humankind. Linked with power, it is the primary gear that governs almost every education program, welfare organization, and rescue/hospice groups. I have to believe that passion and loyalty runs very deep in the passive aggressors because of the common interests in animals. This group tends to stay in it for the "long-haul" because they can actively see where their money and logistical support goes. And, in many cases, these folks still handle the family and business as required; win-win situation for both animals and humans. Additionally, there is strength in numbers and nurture. Most activist or advocates want to participate in meaningful causes with a "team" due to their social nature. Humans are social, as many animals are, and they like to "play together" in the group-support setting, if you will. Therefore, you can have a humane cause, back it up with some "flavor of the month" celebrity, a bunch of "touchy feely" social networking fanatics and you can have dollars coming in from almost every corner of the planet to help save Mr. Silverback Gorilla! . . . Yet again, a win-win situation! Folks if you actually look at it . . . whether it's saving a starving child in a lesser-developed country or a sea turtle, people don't give a damn where the money's coming from. They want help and the passive aggressors are the primary source of funding for many or our rescue and welfare crusades. To even correlate this group with the "apathetic" would be unjust . . . they are usually in fact, the most sympathetic and most effective towards our fight for animal liberation.

The "Obsessive-Compulsive" Woodchucks

Talk about individuals who bite off more than they can chew. I refer to some of these guys as the "semi-self destructive." Their courses of action are like a groundhog constantly gnawing till their teeth wear down; obsessed at the mission with no end in sight. The ups and downs and turmoil are insurmountable. Researchers have always defended the theory that anything in extreme is usually unhealthy physically and emotionally. Consider these same characteristics under the massive umbrella of the Obsessive Compulsive. Though many may hinder the progress, not every "OCD" individual is a detriment to "our" cause if there are controls in place. Perhaps, this will be an opportune way you as typical humans out there can understand why atypical activists do the things they do and why we have such huge burdens to carry. Not all our animal lovin' folks succeed, mind you . . .

Let's say we start off with the obvious . . . A person has been recruited to manage/operate an Animal Hospice in a nonspecific location. He (we will generically use "he") is obsessed with saving every animal on the planet no matter what logistical support he has. On his small, 10acre ranch, he has accumulated 120 dogs, 5 horses, and 2 Llama with 15 volunteers. Blinded to his ability, one man just can't save the world. He, with his oversized heart, has the obsessive need to take on more and more despite the consequences. He did not know when to say enough was enough. As a result, animals become malnourished and neglected both medically and physically. Even within a smaller scope, many are found guilty of taking on too much. Almost everyone knows someone at work or within their social circles, a person falling into this group. In fact, four of the five dogs I share my life with are from a home of this kind. This respectable, co-worker truly loved animals and literally had a zoo of rescued animals (i.e. 2 horses, 4 ferrets, 2 rabbits, 1 goat, 5 dogs, 2 pot-belly pigs, etc. Heck, maybe a partridge in a pear tree? Who knows? Unfortunately, she has a small income and no means to support such a "charitable" undertaking. Added on to this menagerie, "two-legged young-ins", the burden becomes overwhelming thus all suffer the consequences. Rescue groups and private individuals (such as myself . . . smile) had to swoop in and rescue the whole lot . . . for the time! Hoarders of animals are the most dangerous to our animal friends. Here, the focus squarely falls on the diseased individual rather than toward the safety and welfare of the animals. The instance of the "cat lady" down the road found to have 80 cats on the premises is another tragic example. The cats suffer the catastrophic fate while the human is merely treated and diagnosed for her psychological disorder.

Paralleling one of the prior mentioned obsessive woodchucks on our list is our beloved "task wizard." I reluctantly had to place myself into this category. Obsession can take on different set of problems with over-indulging in your passions as activists. Folks rarely understand that people can take on too many projects or tasks and find they are climbing up a waterfall. Nowhere for you to go but down if is it uncontrolled. We have to be realistic and place control barriers on our endeavors so they don't become bigger than life. Saying no is hard when one of your favorite organizations ask for your assistance, yet again and for the hundredth time that month. Since some groups are scarce for their volunteers, they tend to overwork the dedicated few. For example . . . Volunteering and supporting three shelters, helping your community fix fences and doghouses, operating your own website, submitting stories and events in the company bulletin and (whew, getting tired already naming stuff) running around every week exposing bad folks via the video expose' . . . all by yourself/myself makes for a very frustrated and self-destructive human. This is very "mild" example of some folks out there trying to be the super-activists. This individual lives in the "fantasy world", unrealistically believing they alone, can save every living creature. If you don't have the numbers (additional folks or additional support) to achieve sound goals, get them . . . or watch your dreams become a living nightmare. I too, have been there, done that, and ripped up the T-shirt; suffered almost irreversible consequences by over-tasking myself.

Briefly rounding off the lot, we have the compulsive . . . In respect to the animal rights community, the "compulsive" contenders are the short-lived "super-taskers", never finishing what they start. Many may even have the financial and logistical backing on their side but mentally, the "drive" just seems to fade . . . somewhere? These folks join a group, take on a few proverbial "hits" and away they go! Some of our freedom fighters fall into this short-lived category; making a name for themselves and then eventually become bored and seek other adventures; the thrill seekers. The other people heading this category could be the lonely person, usually single, and has no real life and suddenly this idea pops into their head making them feel this will get them somehow noticed. Then they may marry; have twelve kids and "whallah' . . . no more time for those animals! The other folks that seem to fit in this cycle are the spontaneous or "fad" driven crowd, though it primarily encompasses those that are lonely (not always "alone", mind you) or insecure folks. They take on a sporadic "quick fix" or an occupier for the temporary void. We have several of those at my own jobsite.

They get a puppy and suddenly, they realize the focus starts leaning too much on the puppy instead of them and there goes the "wow" affect as fast it came in. The idea of excitement and acceptance certainly didn't lie within the animal's interest. Some people adopt animal companions to fill a void that they may be missing from the human side. Ultimately they decide at some point in time that having that companion doesn't equal to the human attention they actually were seeking. Again, it was self-serving at best. Yes, these are only examples but many know the stinging reality that activist face when the compulsive arrive into the picture. Good, bad or indifferent . . . the healthy activists take on several traits and temper their obsessions with the physical and emotional support of others.

CHAPTER 3

"Breakthroughs" Make for a "Broken Bunny"

Hearing all the experts theorize why animal testing laws don't change, one could speculate that perhaps it is too difficult for the public to understand why activists are agitated or what is actually happening. Several talk about until policies change to stop regarding animals as mere "property", then will  we change our attitudes and practices. "In theory, a six year old could see that logic but in reality . . . everyone must be five because it just "aint" sinking in"! How complicated is that? The excuses we make for our actions, as citizens toward the animal population are alarming. I will discuss a few of the common reasons why we place animals on a "property list" and how this impacts our scientific and social community. Much of our social behavior and interaction with animals can be blamed by humans' need to progress in science and discovery. Some researchers argue if we "test" on the closest living relatives to man (primarily mammals) in the name of research, we will discover and develop more realistic breakthroughs in the treatment of physical and psychological diseases. A more accurate pill created outweighs the livelihood of the beast. However, it certainly does nothing for that chimpanzee or bunny rabbit subjected to pain, suffering, defacement, degradation and enduring outright cruelty until certain destruction/death. Vivisection (broadly defined as any experimentation on live animals) and other forms of animal testing are callously justified in the name of victorious achievements. It is the cruel hierarchy deciding a living mammal's fate. Fix manic depression? Dissect a rabbit's head instead of a human. We either turn a blind eye to the situation because Aunt Suzie's bipolar disorder is regulated now or, we become some raging anarchists and blow up a building and circulate lab rats full of some foreign chemicals onto the community? And since many falsely insist our animal friends feel no pain like humans do, we can boil, choke, and prod at our "property" all day long. It is an ugly picture but a realistic one depicting truth in human behavior. Ultimately, we are contradicting ourselves as human individuals . . . by taking that which we claim most similar to a human and treat them inhumanely as possible. Would I rather use humans to test for new and progressive cures? Yes, indeed . . . rather use the real thing for a more "exact" and factual scientific study than animals . . . reduces hypothesis in research in my book! Strange concept to use animals that aren't vocal in English or any other language to tell a *human* the pain they feel. Obviously a psychopaths' neurology is different from the average human however they are capable of "feeling" pain. Maybe animal abusers should be tested to see if they "feel" physical pain? It is truly amazing that scientists can say animals don't feel pain like we do because of a brain scan-after all, a psychopath brain scan is different but scientists know he "feels" pain because he verbalizes it! Bottom line, we know that animals feel pain!

Related to this problem, is the lack of cognitive reasoning in animals which further subjects our animal kingdom to acts of cruelty. Many laws are predicated on the fact (through scientific study) if animals cannot "reason" . . . they lose rights and "reason" to humanely coexist with our human counterparts; thus the label of "property" is born. It gives farmers, ranchers, "pet owners" (and yes, I hate those two words . . . pet and owner), and hunters all the ammunition they need to go forth and employ their "God-given" property as they see fit. Good, bad or indifferent these behaviors are rarely categorized and if so, minimal progress has been made to protect the animals; farm, domestic, and wild.

CHAPTER 4

Paws'ing to see the "Good" in Technology!

I instinctively want to put a negative spin on everything yet there have been measurable achievements. Sometimes, I find the "Martin's" (pessimist) an easier coping mechanism rather than the optimistic "Pangloss" (from the book . . . "Candide" by Voltair) had depicted in earlier literature. And, if we only dwell on the past, we hinder our forward progression. Nonetheless, we must also learn from history as man did on methods of war. This is a war and until we wake up and realize that all creatures' sufferings and atrocities are worth fighting for, we are no better than the Neanderthal we evolved from. We are super-predators, feeding on the weak when so much progress has been made in the technological and scientific advancement. Hypocrisies, we discover, don't suit mankind as well in today's culture. We are now too egotistical and with that in mind, we have corrected some of our ignorance's. Progression is never a rapid entity. Humans have adopted impatience from technological progress thus, our lazy asses tend to side for instantaneous results. This holds especially true in the animal rights department. I want to find a positive in all of this, possibly helping others in continuing the drive towards peace for all living beings . . .

Laws seldom change but they do and we see many facets of cruelty slowly diminish. Without trying to go through hundreds of platforms we are now using today to expose our wrongdoings and modify bad human behavior, I will generalize on one of them. Technology can be our friend actually in one major capacity . . . the internetsuperhighway! For example, it is a fact; dog fighting is cruel and inhuman. Now, it is illegal throughout our country partly due to exposing and spotlighting these acts via the Internet . . . for every household to finally witness at lightning speeds. Sure, we could be a bit sarcastic claiming it takes some notable case to open folks' eyes but hey, it's a step forward! Additionally, since many countries somehow see us in "the superpower" light (further substantiating our ego trip), we do influence others to some degree to change laws accordingly. All this

is good, not perfect, but good. Media has a huge role in changing our posture in absolutely every imaginable form. Social networks, video websites that upload your own vanities, etc., even emails, chat rooms, and last but not least, our insatiable smart-phones . . . with abilities to reach the world and make us feel connected. This is the by far, one of the greatest advancement and tools for activists' disposal since the Animal Liberation Movements. Though conservatives may argue you have eyeballs in the neighbor's back yard, the positives certainly outweigh the negatives in this instance. We can now show cruelty on our animal friends in lightning speed. One notable case that spread like wildfire through the media was the atrocities in a dairy farm near Cleveland. One of the workers, Billy Joe Gregg, a dairy farm worker of Conklin Dairy Farm, was discovered and charged with 12 counts of cruelty to animals after a welfare group released a video exposing him all over the internet. It shows him and others beating cows with crowbars and poking them with pitchforks. The farm has been extensively publicized in the media all through 2010 and still suspected of atrocities within the organization today. Now we can spread that monster's business all over the planet, busting him and his company to smithereens! Oh, and did we mention the future good it does for the . . . cow. We can bring the circus up close and personal to those folks that hadn't a clue that elephants are being chained and prodded. Whale hunting, polar bears and penguins being squeezed out of their habitat, all these come to reality though you may never stepped a foot on one of these vast countries. It's a reality coming to us at . . . "Google ®" speeds . . . embrace it, growl at it, do as you feel but it's got huge potential to give us faster reaction time by those wanting instant gratification.

CHAPTER 5

I look good, you look good, and then we all look good!

Mankind has so many reasons for why animals are there for social gratification. Whether it's for vanity, sport, super-predator mentality, or profit, the animals are the only species that suffer. Though I talked about scientific "excuses" in an earlier chapter, this one I will focus on the sociological need for mankind to wave his superiority flag.

Vanity is a reason so few people actually notice is taking place in regards to animal welfare. Although there a several examples I can name, some of the most notable are using animals in media and circus performances, sport/game  hunting, and in some instances . . . dog shows. To the average citizen, one can assume these areas are actually a good thing when in fact; all are exercised predominately for exploitation and ego.

At face value, we see the lions, tigers and bears (oh my!) do all these wonderful "eye-catching" feats at a local circus or even on a local television program/commercials. Animals perform for the public to show off their amazing ferocity and tricks. Behind the scenes (witnessed by countless groups), animals are beaten, prodded and ignored. They wait countless hours sitting in some dingy small cage or tethered, barely being cared for or fed. Elephants wait to "wow" their audience while day in and day out; they are chained and subjected to being trained in unnatural feats through acts of torture and negative reinforcement. Organizations responsible for engaging in such horrific acts of violence are many times exposed on national media by activist groups, but repeatedly claim to the public they have stopped these practices. Unfortunately, they go right back to doing these offenses time and time again. Where did you think these captive wild animals are being housed? Even if we dismiss the "unnatural feats" they are forced to perform, they aren't sitting in some nice huge wildlife refuge waiting to go on the next night in front of a filled circus tent or millions of thrill-seekers to watch on the television and video feeds. Scientific research has proven over and over again in thousands of publications, the wild do not do well in captivity and behaviors become increasingly uncontrollable and unpredictable. How many times do we have to see a performer get slaughtered on national TV before we listen to subject matter experts? This "show of exploitation" is nothing more than indulging human's ego and amusement. Sure, this gives way to "profit" as well . . . but basically, the more the public is satisfied, the more revenue it brings in. This furthers man's need for power, greed and selfish vanity.

I can give thousands upon thousands of examples why hunting has become predominately a sport of vanity and power. I'm actually at a loss on where to even begin? . . . Deer, elk, moose, whale, elephant, tiger, you name the wild beast and they are "ripe" for the picking! Hunting enthusiast all over the world are fulfilling huge egos and pockets of revenue all in the name of sport and that magnificent stuffed, dead animal adorning their den walls. Please let's not hide behind hunting for food as a priority . . . . In fact, forgo the consumption side of hunting, and specifically address the massive population of humans (super-predators) doing these acts for mere self-gratification. I can turn on a television and listen to a well publicized hunter go on about the absolute "beauty" and "magnificence "of the beast they gunned down. New and high-power technology allows them even greater force to over-power a beast that never had a single chance to escape the mighty "man". Figurative balls are growing larger and larger as you hear of their exploits in their prideful tones. I am reminded of a typical phrase "they don't even balance the playing field" in the world of hunting. It's obvious they don't even have to . . . "Fight fair", just win.

OMG, how do I lightly tread on the wonderful world of "show? I have some comfort knowing thousands upon thousands of dollars each year  are being contributed to animal welfare by national championship dog shows. In fact, the good "may" outweigh the bad here . . . a sort of "damned if you do, damned if you don't". However, many of the breeders and individual handlers that place dogs in show are the culprits here. Again, countless egos come into play here within all the preparation that goes into the final "walk" in that so publicized arena. Man, do I love to see a beautiful and extraordinary canine in front of my eyes. And to know it sucks that my extreme (ok, obsessive . . . damn) love for canines are showcased in such a fine stature . . . but to what cost? Activists know that many breeders/ trainers crank out hundreds of little puppies to finally produce that one "best in show". Where do all the "other" puppies go? Hmmm, perhaps some are scooted out to adoptions, shelters, a little kid for his birthday or . . . secretly discarded? What little control we have over breeders and trainers hiding many atrocities. I read countless articles of the mayhem that goes on behind the scenes in private facilities (not counting the millions of smaller establishments). We are always looking for that perfect show piece, again to wow our public. I will never discount the hundreds out there who act as responsible breeders and handlers; however, when large cash changes hands and personal ego drives that proverbial train, the animals always take a back seat . . . no matter how you look at. Second, designer and new breeds are popping up almost overnight. Not realizing how these extreme domesticating measures are only yielding weaker, less stable and more dependent species. Is this some secret no one knows about, negative. It's plastered all over the media and written articles. To be fair, in some instances, I do see some more developed breeds but the trade offs, I sense are unbalanced. A "Labra-doodle", a "Malti-poo", whatever new and trendy designer dog that comes through the "mill" are all subjected to disasters both environmentally and socially; too much interference with "mother nature" will ultimate be everyone's (canine and mankind) downfall. More overpopulation, more neglect, more stories to hit the headlines on behalf of human vanity. Does Fluffy really like getting obsessively primped and pushed around like that? Did Sylvester, the "leftover" Boxer, who didn't make the "cut", like it when he was no longer important to his owner? He has just now . . . become nothing but a number or worse, the next one cruelly thrown in the dog fighting arena. Yes, this is from my overall standpoint, but how many activists see this same thing? I am surely not alone in my presumptions, or am I? Surely you jest!

The final area (I know just know I will "step in it) . . . the massive production and consumption of "meat". I know there will never be some spontaneous change of conscience in humanity and the world will not just stop eating animals and manufacturing animal by-products. One would be living in a pure fantasy world. I'm not even going to tread on how going the "vegan" way would benefit all. I too, struggled from the weak instinct to be carnivorous every single day. Let's me say that we need to gradually change our perception of farm and wild animals. We raise millions of pounds of live flesh to cut them short in the name of "chowing down" and designer footwear. We are not some starving mountain man, foraging every day for food. If we are wealthy enough to afford all this high tech gear and advancements in technology to gun down a deer or slaughter a baby lamb for condoms, then I think we should be giving a little bit more consideration in our

actions as a modern society. As touchy of a subject as this is, I'm not going to say we don't all have own devils to tackle. I do know that slowly there are anticruelty movements and changes in technology that are decreasing the onslaught; however it is an overwhelming painstaking feat. Combating the inhumanities involved in these processes is our first priority in the protection of farm and wild animals. It's not a "kill or be killed" situation any more. I don't see a "cave man" mentality necessary when all these advances in research, technology and synthetic processes are great supply. Working on the problem has already been found to be an extensive challenge that we need very high focus on. In between, I'm still good with "smacking down" fur coat lovers, panther-piss harvesters and ivory adorners. It takes all groups and in every location (numbers make the fight more effective) so I say we individually grab what handful of causes we can manage effectively and continue recruiting children and their parents to instill better morals for future livelihoods. Advocates continue pushing for more education programs, orchestrate demonstrations and rallies, and even support the freedom fighters, thus all have a place in society in combating all forms of abuse. I will outline some suggestions to move effectively forward in a later chapter. We (activists) aren't some gods but we certainly are going to continue to "move mountains" trying!

CHAPTER 6

Talking to elephants, mice and even sloths

Whether we are trying to convey our message to big elephant ears, or small mice ears, sympathetic or those with sloth like attitudes, all individuals are important in getting the point across. Trying

to outline some simple process on teaching others animal welfare is a bit of a frustrating yet necessary task. Experts have many ways towards approaching the public. I will try to give you some personal methods that have either worked for me or with one of my neighboring advocate friends. The first thing is to outline a course of action. Within that, I tackle the "who, what, when and where's encompassing the "how to" throughout the entire process. This is only a suggestive approach and will be quite intensive and adaptive as situations change. It is a common and practical way I use to spread the message of non-human animal welfare to humans. Your course of action must also work around your specific audiences . . . target audience, if you will. This makes a crucial difference in how you are going to interject your ideology in positive and effective manner. As a long time leader among soldiers (military retired) I have faced many obstacles in teaching to the target audience. Some factors to consider in your audiences would be age, education/position level, background, and environment/setting. A number of of these groups have a tendency to parallel each other and gives way to using a combination of teaching approaches. It logically comes to play when outlining your individual courses of action. Each factor determines your teaching method as I will show here . . .

Teaching children on animal welfare must be approached far differently than adults. Compassion and empathy must be taught. Incorporating simple acts of kindness and respect in the teaching of our children to protect even the smallest of creatures may develop lasting values towards one another; thus preventing many forms of human and non-human animal violence. Many well known, high profile organizations and local shelters have shown time and time again, documented proof that children naturally identify respect through teaching our children to protect even the smallest of creatures. Even the simple act of bringing a small animal into the class environment and allowing them to interact with the animal can teach valuable lessons. Additionally children respond extremely well to therapy involving dogs and cats or even horses and rabbits. People bring them to the hospitals for children to brighten their spirits. It has been proven through countless publications and social research facilities that rehabilitation is faster with animal therapy.

We must also considerchildren's young minds; realize that "kids" scare quite easily. Throwing some tales of horror at them might not be  the most advisable approach. Children will always be impressionable and whatever we do, they will mimic our actions. If their parents have been chaining their 5 year old Rottweiler in the back yard for the majority of his life, the kids might not have too many feelings on the matter. Informative literature coupled with positive words to the young may somehow influence their parents to "modify" their behaviors. In fact, this one act of compassion is a huge step in creating a better life for their animal companion. Let's use this very simple situation since I brought this up. If I want to teach a bunch of grade-school kids on the benefits of *not* chaining their dog outside; emphasizing the positive rather than the negative things of Rover, the Rottweiler standing out there would be crucial. I may want to use their compassions to my advantage. If I approach little Gregory and exclaim, "If Rover is inside a fence instead of chained up to that tree all day, he can run around and play and chase all the squirrels and keep his family safe too. Wouldn't you like that?" Now if I stated that same phrase as "if you don't let Rover loose from that cruel metal chain and allow him to roam and come inside, he will suffer both mentally and physically with no means to defend himself from predators and human cruelties . . . etc.", you will lose him. Through this strategy I will be simultaneously reaching out (indirectly) to the parents/caregivers. Parents and kids alike don't want threats and proverbial "attacks" thrown at them. So the positive and meticulous approach with "choosing your words" carefully will be the healthier route to take in this situation. Additionally, some horrifying pictures or movies will certainly do more harm than good. Mommy may get terribly mad at you if you barked at a kid and said his mom and dad are torturing their dog. Somehow, I don't see that approach going so well; consequences will arise. It's like telling a kid to eat his carrots because it will make him see rather than saying to him that if he doesn't eat carrots he will become vitamin deficient and go blind. Fun and interactive illustrations and media truly get your point across and at the appropriate age level! Again, we don't show "horror" to a five year old! Most of this is logical however; the toughest thing to control is personal feelings. Keep it positive to motivate them . . . if you don't, you lose mom, dad, guardians and the impressionable kiddies!!!

In line with this, we have to consider the education level and positions your target audience holds. If you are pushing for tougher laws within your community and have the city council staring down your face, your approach would be different than perhaps a group of college students, a five year old or maybe that neighborhood watch group. Coupled with that, you have individual's education and background levels to deal with. Talk with the audience' level rather than down to them. This also means not talking above their heads. As with some of the other groups, if you have to address those dreaded council members, do not automatically throw your personal feelings into the presentation. Use what I call the "bottom line" approach. Describe the problem up front, the negative impacts on the animal welfare and the recommended solutions to create, amend or abolish a law. Then go a step further and provide your members supporting arguments within a brief booklet of facts or suggestions that they can take with them for further study. Always give solutions that have been proven to work by your neighboring counties or states to help reduce or eliminates some form of animal abuse, etc. Since this group is already prepared to bombard you with criticism in almost every case, you have to be ready to support your argument with intelligent resilience and in a very structured format.

If you are asked to promote animal welfare at a college campus, you may want to interject a "wow" effect (as I call it) here, and

perhaps a personal experience (some ice-breakers). Let's say for example . . . Let's say, if I was to speak on the cruelties within the cattle industry, I may want to tell a true "story" of a very dramatic event that recently appeared in current events. This gives your audience to get their brains into your conversation instead of their smart phones. I have more time for audience attention and stage presence. I would also throw some satirical relief within my program. You really have to get these guys' attention! Dramatic and interesting media support along with perhaps some physical props could really "wow" your audience in a very positive way. Not unlike kids, they love stimulation but on their level now. I strongly suggest you show very careful consideration on how many or to what degree of atrocities (if any) you want to show to them as well. Too graphic can lead to incitement or even lose your audience to withdrawal or fear. You motivate more folks with positives than you do with graphic horrors. In some venues, this may be effective, however, choose those times very wisely!!! You also may have more "face time" with college students than perhaps those city council hard-heads. Council members haven't the time or patience and want things straight to the point. College students are impressionable, risk takers and hungry for knowledge; use these attributes to your advantage. They are also in the age of technology. This is yet another tactic you should use to your advantage; if used appropriately. I do this many times on different websites and electronic bulletin boards. A lot of college students along with typical "media junkies" tend to like that "stimulation" of dramatic and perhaps rhythmic uploads while mixing things up with humor that will tactically get the message across. On another side of the spectrum, don't offer up some "quick fix" that cannot be realistically accomplished; basically no B.S. Anyone can read through an ignorant or incompetent instructor. Don't push off some "unsubstantiated" rhetoric that's going to lose your credibility either. Remember these are college kids. I would side with an intellectual stimulation paired with a charismatic approach.

What about targeting those "subject matter experts" (SME'S) or "advocate" group? Now this is where I "call out" my own crew; they love preaching to the choir. Depending on what you are trying to teach this type of audience, you can find yourself going nowhere and quick. Did you recruit more supporters and/or activists or did you just corral the same numbers of folks that were already sympathetic to our cause and push them to action.

Don't fall into this trap of educating the educated. The most preferred venue you should be using with fellow activists are how they, themselves can go out and teach their material to the uneducated population; train-the-trainer! The worse thing I can think of is getting all this propaganda thrown at me that I already know. Give me tools to teach the uneducated. You can sit there all day and "hoop and holler" with your group of already sympathetic activists but that huddle will never spread out and become viral. We (activists) don't even mind hearing of the experiences and personal success stories or freedom fighter escapades but when I (an avid activist) open up my unnamed "social site" or emails and see all these tons of videos on "why vivisection is cruel" or "the dairy farm atrocities", either someone is just "mass spamming" me or most likely they weren't targeting their audience very well. Strangely enough, this happens to me all the time. And, this is more common than we care to admit. Another important area to focus the activists on is updates and changes to law and new and innovative developments that help their particular cause. This is where I want others teach me on! Don't tell me Mr. Elephant is being cruelly exterminated for his tusks; tell me what are the new developments being done to make this practice illegal. Quick referencing of the topics is fine, in fact, a bit of history doesn't deter from the intent. Remember, though, we need to stay on point and focus towards a mission.

Talking to the indifferent or badly informed group is a particular challenge to the overzealous activists. Also, bear in mind, those "one on one" or "small groups" that may "own" animals can be very dangerous if not approached effectively. For example if approached very directly with "guns blazing", he or she may hide the cruelties he may be inflicting upon his animal companions rather than work on fixing the problem. I find resorting to the instinctive "hitting below the belt" may or may not work with this particular group. Your tactics play and primary role in getting the message out to those who, in the activists mind may, quite frankly, mistakenly believe and not care! These are not the "apathetic" crew. These are the misinformed and ignorant. Although, my first instinct is to "beat them down" with an aggressiveness sad tale, but it is only going to make them escape off into never-never land. Worst case scenario, it has a very negative impact on the defenseless animals placed in their charge. I know . . . we can rescue the poor fellahs and then beat them (humans) down? Unfortunately, that isn't an option either! Damn.

As far as your neighbors, they may also be taken back if you hit them with "scare tactics". I won't say that in some situations, that wouldn't work but for a novice out there, this may not be your first course of action. I like to share a simple tactic I used in approaching a neighbor with a simple canine situation due to my years of experience in dealing with canine welfare. Now, you can take this technique and apply it to many different situations. However, you must bear in mind that any tactical approach must change as the situation changes . . . positive results, you need to slack off, less or negative results need a change in strategy. I am just presenting a typical case in the example below. You can get a general idea on how to teach with tact and control. It actually worked on several occasions with me and with positive results . . .

Case in point: Let's say you are approached by a fellow companion to our animal friends with confronting a nearby neighbor that may be suspected of mistreating or neglecting a family dog. We MISTAKINGNLY want to react with aggressive and ineffective means. You initially come upon your young neighbor that has a somewhat skinny dog chained outside with no shelter and water bowl knocked over and no chew toys in the area, etc.

Your role: Let us not forget that you need to be very certain of the accusations and the severity of situation(s). This means EVALUATE first!! How long has the dog been outside? Was the dog just placed out there recently due to other reasons (repairs, awaiting containment, etc.)

Do you truly know the particular animal in question is being abused or neglected? Or, is this a common case of over-reacting by initial and distant observation . . . on your part? Are you privy to all the facts, not mere assumptions? Did the neighbor across the street by some reason or another just inherit this unexpected pooch and is uneducated on the proper treatment and care of this newfound friend. Heck, this dog may be a previous boyfriend/girlfriend's, their mother-in-law's dog, an abandoned dog, etc. Too many people jump first and don't truly investigate. Finding out the dog is in not as severe of a situation as previously assumed, you should delve into the next step . . . EDUCATE the neighbor with tact and positive motivational techniques. It is always your responsibility to educate regardless of who the dog belongs to. Some ideas could be dropping by and soliciting your services and expertise with assisting your neighbor or solicit a fellow resident expert on the matter to handle it for you. By being inquisitive, using kind words and a tactical approach to the matter, you may find that the owner of this bundle of joy has such been placed in this newfound situation and has no clue on raising or protecting his new "roommate". So, tread lightly and investigate, then give helpful solutions and aid where you can. Play an active role in helping with the developing constructive solutions. Some examples may include construction of safe shelters or containment areas, educating your neighbor on nutritional needs, socialization and so on. Temporarily volunteer to assist during the down times or even while things are put into place for them. After these measures are taken, "slack off on the involvement" and then observe at a distance. So, next we want to MONITOR at a distance within reason, legal limitations, and with common sense.

"Save a Dog..."

Save a dog from...

•Shelters... lonely, confined, and in need of socialization; desperate for human companionship and compassion

•Chains...neglected, abused, vulnerable to elements and attacks with nowhere to run for protection from harm's way

•Confinement...crated and caged for hours on end, forgotten and regarded as property with no real place to call home or a real someone to be called "friend"

•Dogfights...cruel, abusive and immoral, yet practiced widely and ignored by many who consider themselves "citizens of the community"

•Puppy Mills...sold off as a mere "commodity", a "thing" used for profit and living in constant dismal conditions; camouflaged in the name of capitalism

•Ignorance...the uneducated and the unwilling humans who see their dogs as "property"; denied the right for a better quality of life

•Extinction...a life deprived of natural instincts to roam, socialize and play; a desire to be characterized as a dog and not a showcase for self-serving human vanity

•Inhumanities... exploitation, marketing tools and public spectacles; marked only for status, ratings, financial investment, and/or profit margins

Save a Dog... The humanity you show for a dog may not change the world...but it will change the world for that ONE dog!

I want to strongly caution the OBSESSIVE (oh, I'm sorry . . . are you looking at me?!?) animal lovers out there though . . . the way others treat their animals may not be to your stringent standards (as my standards often are) but still be just as loving and appropriate. In other words, you may sleep with your dogs and other owners have them lying on a dog bed in the den. Both dogs may be just as loyal and happy.

Each situation calls for individual design . . . all for complimenting the animal's instinct, capabilities, breed, purpose, and environmental factors. The other extremely important thing to remember is . . . if you "reasonably" suspect any animal abuse in your neighborhoods (dog, cat, rabbit, cows, horses, etc.), REPORT THE ABUSE TO LAW ENFORCEMENT! Even if they have to watch a suspected "wrongdoer", they will initiate a "paper trail" and will start documenting history on the culprit. You have a stronger case if this individual had a past record of abuse. Maybe that domestic animal will be re-homed to a more loving environment due to your actions. Doing nothing may lead to abuse or death.

What about teaching to the apathetic individual(s); those who actually have been programmed not to ever care about our animal friends? There are those who go about treating them as insignificant property no matter what positive or proactive mechanics you put in place. If the laws don't cover the suspected infraction, then the group that needs focusing on is local and state governments. Additionally focus on the places that don't have local protection laws. This takes support throughout your communities. There are always going to be groups that will never change their attitudes and practices. Since we can't shoot them legally, we have to resort to the only actions available within the law. Perhaps, this is why those freedom fighters are always popping up. And this is why we have our activists on constant alert for those wrongdoers and report abuse throughout the public information highway to thwart off these abusers and rescue the few that they can. I also have extreme difficulties in correcting sociopathic predators. I will say, however, I use a number of people and my networking skills to my advantage here with some success. I can't reach out to all apathetic individuals. I do know that if everyone starts from local neighborhoods and spread out, we can at least change their kids' perception of humane treatment. By also reaching out to the specialized groups, we can further take aggressive actions toward the "deaf" and nonconformists who are both funded and logistically supported by area supporters. I support both advocates and activists to better spread the power throughout all areas worldwide. Groups that target specific area such as whale slaughtering are effective. Then you have those who take actions against poachers, sport hunters, and furriers, etc. That's why we have varieties of folks with an assortment of causes. One individual can only do so much in his fight. So, don't shoot them, my friends . . . just hope they get eaten by the very prey they inhumanely slaughter or terrorize!

Last but not least, another group is that popular friendship network. This forum can be a great communication link to educate if done tactfully and sporadically. Here again, don't post some horrifying videos on your favorite social networking venue to all your friends' list to attempt to get your message across either. Second, if you post every day some horrible and sad story of some un-adopted furry companion, you may find you'll be "ex-friended" very quickly. Suddenly, there disappear your hundreds of potential supporters in the future. For your "garden variety" friends, be sparingly and conservative. Keep your uploaded material mild, informative and submit subject matter that will appeal to their sense of right and wrong; conscience as caring human beings. If you are going for the "fear factor", consider which audiences you are targeting on your network of friends. The primary thing for all activists is to recruit new humanitarians by using positive teaching tools for them to use in their future journey.

Every course of action you take to promote animal welfare, no matter how small your feat, you *save at least one other living creature from certain harm*. We cannot just turn our backs on the innocent, loving and loyal animals that have no voice of their own. Second, every act will never have one hundred percent effectiveness. I wish every action I've taken (verbal, non-verbal, direct or indirect) has all positive outcomes. I can't lead every human or animal rights cause out there but to contribute some way in my daily life, I know it may spark a chain reaction to those who I did reach out there. Teaching is difficult, however, if you live by example and have a true passion for what you are teaching in, it becomes far easier than you think! I live to discover new and effective ways to combat animal cruelty and learn to use the tools I have to make it work for each situation I come across. I may lose sometimes. I may win on occasion. The primary thing to remember is that I try . . . that's what really counts, for them.

CHAPTER 7

Your character-base; luck doesn't have a thing to do with it

This would have to be one of my favorite subject areas . . . establishing and understanding *your* "character-base". Now mind you . . . this is NOT a group method of attack as we discussed in our "Methodology" chapter. This is how you as a teacher interact with your "students" or listeners. I learned these "behavior" traits from an old primary leadership development course (PLDC) I attended years ago as a young sergeant in the army. It stuck with me all throughout my life. To lead a group (troops) to battle and teach them what they need to know, you must understand your power and base your character around these parameters. Methodology is one thing but your *"personal"* character base is something we all have to understand in order to teach others about animal welfare. Three primary character bases I will touch base on will be represented by an animal that takes on the similarities I want to convey. It adds an easier and humorous tenor to my explanation. I literally observe each of these models practiced every day of my life, either as a "civilian" or while serving twenty years as a soldier so I'm well versed in seeing their effectiveness in play. This time, I will use the Hippopotamus, the Koala Bear and the Labrador. Obviously I love using animals as my illustrations . . .

The **Hippopotamus** will be our first character

base. Now hold on, I love ALL animals. The Hippo just happens to be one of the most aggressive . . . Ha! This individual uses his power over his subjects to get the mission accomplished . . . bottom line. No matter the cost, it will be accomplished. The primary objective is to engage the target and attack! Hit below the belt to get maximum effectiveness. Those who use the "autocratic" or "authoritative" power or character base may or may not hit the target! You may actually scare away your audience(s) or intimidate them to pretty well pacify your "demands". Teaching is an art but without tactically approaching your "subjects" without shredding them in the process may not achieve a freaking thing. I want you to teach them, not eat them alive! A proverbial "dead" human is of no use to the animal community and their sustainment. Additionally, a "Hippo" approach to teaching doesn't always mean he or she knows what he's talking about or has been kept up-to-date on all the strategies within his grasp. A Hippo attacks with fervor, and so does the aggressive, BMOC (big man on campus) with more attention to himself rather than the cause at hand. Why would an authoritative leader teach all what he knows? Many authoritative teachers and leaders tend to hoard some of their innovative and educative strategies to keep the light on themselves. The objective here is . . . the more you know in preventing animal cruelty, the more that apprentice or individual needs to know on his battle to wipe out animal suffering. If I know how to build a better battleship . . . damn it, I want others to build one too! And, I want them to use it! Don't be selfish and keep all the "meat" to yourself. As my ole chief (CW3 Gonzales) used to say to me . . ." I don't want you to be as good as me! I want you to be better!"

The **Koala Bear** . . . ah, this is the "charmer" who works the crowd and has the charisma to match. The Koala can be useful to some degree and some not . . . One area the charismatic approach is advantageous is utilizing notable figureheads, famous celebrities or some cute man or woman as your spokesperson to "assist" in your cause. Sure, the Bottled-nosed Dolphins may not

give a crap how some "hottie" (male or female) looks in your educational brochures or even standing up on the podium. I guarantee one thing . . . the monies you make while you charm the audience may bring in more resources to protect that fine sea mammal! Whatever publicity stunt will work in providing some defenseless creature shelter and food, I say . . . tactics are tactics. If you got it, flaunt it and if it saves a life in the process, you are golden!!!

Now, there is the bad side to this "cutie" if teaching with no background on the subject matter! You will lose your audience just as quick with a hippo as you will with a koala if the facts don't add up. If you stand before a crowd of a hundred and want to talk about the changes in tethering laws, for example, you need to know your subject as well. Don't assume all humans are shallow. Additionally, don't assume your "dumb blonde" characteristics will get these folks out to vote for your cause and contribute in some way without giving solid facts and figures. Folks, "stupidity" will eventually leach to the top and all you will be left with is people more concerned with your cuteness and forget what the primary objective was. Never let your audiences become so mesmerized and forget to take back the lessons you want to convey. We are all about moving forward no matter how small the steps. I don't want to see you taking giant leaps backwards; doing more harm than good!

The last one I will discuss is the **Labrador Retriever.** This is certainly the most effective since he uses a combination of styles to work with . . . versatility, power, charisma, and brains! An unmatched compilation of endurance and capabilities all wrapped up in a durable package to boot. The Labrador has been always known for the diversity they display. Not only do they represent one of the highest IQ's around, they are smart hunters, family companions, cute, and agile. I'd follow this guy anywhere! We can use all these "lab" traits to win over several audiences . . . the ignorant, the apathetic and the intelligent. The healthier combination of characteristics you swallow up in your teaching styles, the more future activists, supporters and compassionate citizens (caring human animals) you turn loose on society while systematically achieving your goals.

Ok, now that you know which "category", you may fall into, how do go about using your personal character base effectively? For example, if you are that Hippo or Koala, what do you do to modify your behavior? YOU MUST EDUCATE YOURSELF on all aspects of what you are teaching on. Having that combination "lab" character base is optimal but must be developed. Knowledge is learned powers . . . go get it! And . . . it's free! If you have all the brains and no charisma, seek folks to help you to work that magical influence on others and "partner up" in stomping out cruelty! I have "aggressive" components in my personality if told honestly. I have great teaching skills but my lack of control with certain groups is often my biggest challenge. Therefore, I constantly train myself control techniques and get others recruit ted to help with my weakness. Let others out there compliment your character so you have a strong chain of support. Know your limitations and go out and train yourself to be better in your teaching skills. To get the public's attention, sometimes you have to be a bit more intelligent in your approach and not always think your charm or "military discipline" alone will win them over!

CHAPTER 8

"Housetraining" your Humanitarians

We went through all these stages of developing "our" (you and me) animal lovers into productive "activist" and followers, now we have to ensure  our "house" is in order as well. There is nothing worse than going over to one of my fellow animal lovers and find their personal and physical house in complete disarray. You can't teach others and expect them to retain good habits if you don't set the example! OMG, can this be one of the toughest things to fix yet the simplest task of all? A few of the things you need to "clean up" then is at a personal level. The three I will discuss is the physical, financial and . . . wait for it . . . verbal and non-verbal. I'll explain in detail below . . .

First let's delve into the physical role of the activist or future followers. I don't mean requiring some physical workout program. Heck that would be quite hypocritical on my part . . . smile! We aren't talking of a PT program folks so don't run away. I mean getting your own house in order in respect to cleanliness and healthiness. One way is to ensure your environment is *safe* for all habitats. How will you be an effective "leader" if you fall short in this arena? You must ensure safe refuge such as fencing and proper size containment for the specific breed/ or species. Additionally, you must keep a reasonably clean environment for both you and your furry and not-so-furry friend's health. You can't be a slob, have fleas all over your dogs, crap in the yard from 2002 and expect this to be a suitable living environment. How do this make you look? Well, it definitely sheds a very poor light on you as a proactive and reputable representative to your cause(s). If my dogs (I have pooches), for example weren't spayed/neutered, had unkempt coats, didn't get regular vet checks, and my house smelled of 30 day old pee-pee, I can kiss my reputation "bye-bye". Once that word got out I'm a hypocritical slob, the whole animal AND non-animal loving community would throw me "under the bus".

I must maintain my own house and responsibilities with my own four-legged family members to teach good practices to our youth or uninformed public. One of my colleagues I mentioned previously with the entire "zoo" on her premises has a habit of bad housecleaning; unhealthy and unsafe for all the creatures concerned! In fact, if you wanted to get a rescued critter from that residence, I assure the vet bills will be much more than you opted . . . i.e. flea and tick control, shots that were "outdated", various worms, etc. Sure, I can expect some issues to come with a rescue but if they were in your charge for some length of time, some of those issues should not be a concern. Whatever your cause or fight is, shouldn't you follow suit with your objectives? Would you "chain up" your dog outside and have improper shelters on the premises and teach others of the inhumanities of long-term tethering? I would think not!

The next area we should focus on is the financial responsibility. We touched on this a "smidgen" when we talked about the "over-taskers" and such. However, we are focusing here on your personal finances. Nothing worse than having too many animals running around your house and they don't have proper nutrition and supplements. If you can't afford having the six camels in your back yard, consider downsizing so their health and wellbeing won't suffer from your lack of financial accountability. No one says that temporary setback due to unforeseen situations are a lack of responsibility on your part. Everyone goes through some downfalls. I am focusing on the ones that decide or become preemptive and adopt or take on another animals' care and can't even take care of themselves. Oh, you know the ones I speak of. Many folks out there unfortunately fall into this category. They care but don't understand the responsibilities of . . . proper caring! These folks we try to convince them to donate to causes instead of say . . . buying the horse and you haven't a way to take care of it. Know your limitations and means! Oh, and be realistic and get your head out of the clouds. You are, again, not super-human! How would it look if I have my own family of five eating some "cheapy" kibble, no updated shots due to lack of income and . . . I preach to you today of maintaining a safe and healthy environment for our animal friends? Again, a strike against me in the worst way!

Last but folks, I will never claim the least . . . the most difficult hurdle to climb . . . the verbal and nonverbal maintenance (what I like to call it). How many times do I watch or see many of my animal

lovers and activists on websites or other forms of media and cuss at the world or to another when they are disgruntle. I guarantee the only thing the public will remember you by is your mouth! It can get you in trouble more than you know. I will make a very simple example of comparison . . . Say we have two well known activist invited to speak on a talk show about puppy mills on different channels. One becomes irate; yelling and cursing obscenities and getting downright nasty and confrontational. The other, however, doesn't take things "personal", maintains a professional demeanor, stays calm during challenging questions and sticks to supporting arguments. Who will you side with? You may remember that individual that made a complete "ass" of themselves but will you be inclined to follow his/ her "teachings?" The majority of the public hates a spectacle. I do for that fact. I can't say I don't use "colorful metaphor" on occasion, but in public is never a place to do this. Yes, in most settings it is inappropriate. We are all not perfect, mind you. You see this also on the web. Unfortunately some of my favorite activists out there and go absolutely ridiculous; publicize their disappointments across the World Wide Web in a very derogatory manner. One in particular had apparently "ratted" this group out for some type of event so that person cussed them all up and down right on the site . . . wow, I think that could have been done a bit more professionally or even dealt with on a "private" level. I could have thought of a hundred alternatives to deal with that "traitor", if you will . . . smile.

Ok, so your nonverbal could be simple things such as posture, dress, and actions that you have absolutely no idea your doing wrong. Very simple example of this was what I saw on television one day . . . A vet came on a news program discussing domestic animal care. He was dressed nicely; however, he became visibly annoyed with the pooch sitting on his lap because, what looked to be, he was getting hair on him? What? This is an animal caregiver! Hello! Though amusing, I seen the non-verbal cues here . . . at least "I" wouldn't take my "smoochy-poochies' to see him! It's just the impression he gave off; nothing he actually said. Another example is the protestors that want to physically get rude in public. No, I'm not referring to our freedom fighters that do things in covert. I'm talking about the hell raiser shown on the "channel nine news" that raised that proverbial finger or basically . . . "showed his ass" on national TV. Perhaps some setting may call for a bit of "theatrics" but to embarrass yourself on a national media may not be the message we want to send the public out. FOCUS ON THE REAL ISSUE . . . THE ANIMALS!!! It is NOT about YOU! Just remember that when you lose your reputation, you sit as the lone hyena with no "pack" in the fight! Work as the situation calls for but maintain some verbal and non-verbal control. No one is perfect but work on it and do the best you can!

CONCLUSION

I suppose everything is disputable no matter how many times things are tried and tested. Many of my views I share are opinionated and have been assessed through trial and error all in the name of animal liberation. I've also taken ideas from those average citizens out there that I've either admired or despised throughout my many years and learned better strategies in combating animal cruelty worldwide. I would never profess to be an expert by any means. I do know, I've experienced so much and will continue learning every waking day. I've actually practiced these theories and want to give folks out there the tools that seemed to work for me. I took my own experiences and tried to compile them to a simpler mode. You also must know, all is not a perfect, straightforward path and you will slip and fall during your travels and teachings. The primary thing is for everyone to at least try. Never stop teaching and being a good example for others to emulate is paramount. Bear in mind, you must always know that it takes more than one technique/method and a many super comrades to help further our crusade. One superhero does great . . . Tens of thousands magnify our effort and will help even greater!

After writing about some of my successes and failures and giving what little novice advice I can to folks out there on animal rights, has my overall disposition changed for the better? Has this been therapeutic? I know that wasn't my primary objective, I will say that! I suppose it's all in how you look at. I still cry when I hear the circus coming to town or if an innocent creature lay dead in the road. I continue using colorful profanities and metaphors toward those apathetic to our cause. I still run into brick walls trying to educate the public to take animals off of the "property list". I push for world peace and animals to be included in our humanitarian progression. I relentlessly squeeze in countless hours toward fighting for animal liberation. Twenty years in the military and enduring countless hardship tours and conflicts, did the "drill sergeant" tour and even jumped out of airplanes . . . but nothing compares to the hardships of convincing others to change their attitudes toward another human or non-human animal. You must still "rock on" for their sake. If you really look at from the standpoint of who's "feelings" and livelihood I'm concerned with anyway, I will tell you this . . . . It's always been about them . . . the animals; domestic, farm and wild. Animal liberation must equal human liberation . . . And that's really all that matters to me anyway!

"The greatness of a nation and its moral progress can be judged by the way its animals are treated."
Mahatma Gandhi

The End

Quotes and Folks

"He is your friend, your partner, your defender,
your dog.
You are his life, his love, and his leader.
He will be yours, faithful and true to the last beat of
his heart.
You owe it to him to be worthy of such devotion."
Author Unknown

" . . . Until the last abuse has ceased
and existence is granted to every beast
We won't abandon or give in
because this war we intend to win"
Janet Riddle

The worst sin towards our fellow creatures is not to hate them, but to be indifferent to them. That's the essence of inhumanity. George Bernard Shaw

---

V. Mezzatesta

Our task must be to free ourselves . . . by widening our circle of compassion to embrace all living creatures and the whole of nature and its beauty. Albert Einstein

---

Until one has loved an animal, a part of one's soul remains unawakened. Anatole France

---

Mankind's true moral test, its fundamental test (which lies deeply buried from view), consists of its attitude towards those who are at its mercy: animals. And in this respect mankind has suffered a fundamental debacle, a debacle so fundamental that all others stem from it.

Milan Kundera, *The Unbearable Lightness of Being*

I don't believe in the concept of hell, but if I did I would think of it as filled with people who were cruel to animals. Gary Larson

---

"Animals' worse threats are predators not of the animal kind but of the human . . ."

V. Mezzatesta

The indifference, callousness and contempt that so many people exhibit toward animals is evil first because it results in great suffering in animals, and second because it results in an incalculably great impoverishment of the human spirit. Ashley Montagu

---

If you have men who will exclude any of God's creatures from the shelter of compassion and pity, you will have men who will deal likewise with their fellow men. St. Francis of Assisi

---

The Animals of the planet are in desperate peril. Without free animal life I believe we will lose the spiritual equivalent of oxygen. Alice Walker

---

The humanity you show for a dog may not change the world . . . but it will change the world for that ONE dog! Author unknown

---

If you think you have 1st Amendment Rights, you are sadly misled . . . You have rights only when it suits "human causes", not animals! V. Mezzatesta

---

ABOUT THE AUTHOR

 Born February 1961 from Italian parents, I was adopted and came to the U.S. in 1964. Never fitting into that mold predetermined by my family and found I done everything in my power to go "against the grain" and become a rebel as a young adult. Raised from abuse, I grew up to be oversensitive to any forms of abuse but still led a very structured and ordered life. After retirement from the military, I received a B.S. degree (Troy University) in Social Sciences; majoring in Sociology. My interests in the science of human behavior drifted into the desire to understand our animal friends as well.

Strangely enough my "renegade" mentality had great influence on my direction toward becoming an activist later on. I started with private rescue of canines after retirement. I wrote local literature on canine welfare and continue assisting outlying communities in various projects. I graduated toward the need to broadcast and educate nationally; founded a site related to liberation and activism in the defense of all animals—domestic, farm and wild. I also fight to abolish words such as "*property, pets* and *ownership*" when relating to animals. I have represented my community in advocating for anti-tethering and spaying/neutering of domestic animals and regarded as a canine consultant. I've done limited guest spots on one of our local media stations and considered as a well regarded advocate. My entire life is modified around my interactions with our animal companions. My family consists of one 2-legged daughter and five 4-legged kids. I am against treating animals like some "circus" clowns or puppets so all of mine are only "housetrained" and nothing else . . . just get to be . . . dogs!

Currently I work in city government. I plan to leave this line of work one day to fulfill my destiny; full time work in animal welfare. Although this job has truly taught me my limitations as an activist, I find these "restrictions" have me too confined thus need to broaden my horizons into the field I truly had a "calling" to . . . animal liberation. I live each day to find better ways to inform our public of the inhumanities and work to circumvent some of the problems by my words, action and deed.

V. Mezzatesta